Through God's Eyes

Through God's Eyes

EIGHT TRUTHS TO HELP YOU RISE FROM VICTIMHOOD TO VICTORY

BARBARA PEREZ

Printed in the United States of America
ISBN: 979-8-9870898-0-4
Published By: Barbara Perez
Cover and Layout Design: Barbara Perez
Editing By: The Creative Me

This book is dedicated to Debbie and Poncho.
I pray you always see yourselves through God's eyes
and live a victorious life

You must be cautious, because making your life better means adopting a lot of responsibility, and that takes more effort and care than living stupidly in pain and remaining arrogant, deceitful, and resentful.

DR. JORDAN B. PETERSON

CONTENTS

INTRODUCTION

A VISIT TO THE DOCTOR IS IN ORDER

Some people believe that when you accept Jesus in your heart, all your hurt, pain, hang-ups, addictions, and everything else is automatically fixed. It seems that for a long time, this was (and perhaps still is) the message of the church. Please, don't misunderstand me. It is true that when we give our lives to Jesus, our lives are transformed. After all, this means that our sins are forgiven, and we have the promise of eternal life. But what it doesn't mean is that everything in our lives is immediately fixed. God is all powerful and He can, if He wishes, fix things immediately. But I find that for most people, healing is a process. We can spend our entire life in the process.

And this is an important concept to understand,

because many of us can become disillusioned when we realize that there are still things in us that need fixing. We still have injuries and scars from past experiences that are affecting us in the present. This doesn't make our walk and experience with Jesus any less real. In fact, it makes us more dependent on Him because we certainly can't walk this flawed life on our own. We need Him to walk alongside us, to guide us, to comfort us, and to lead us towards a complete life with Him.

This book was not easy to write. I was very hesitant to expose my struggles. After all, I have been a Christian for many, many years. I was embarrassed to share that after all these years I am still needing daily help. Embarrassed that there are still areas in my life where I need Jesus more than ever. Embarrassed that I might need to reach out for help. But during this journey, I have discovered that God, in His infinite love, has left many amazing tools that can help us in our walk and in our path toward healing.

Think of burn victims. Burns are typically classified into degrees. A first-degree burn is one that only affects the outer layer of the skin. Imagine someone who gets burned while cooking. Depending on the severity of the burn, he might just need to cool the burn, apply a wet compress, and apply some type of antibiotic ointment. Within a couple of weeks, your skin may be back to normal.

A second-degree burn happens when the outer layer as well as the layer underneath have been damaged. You might see red blisters that hurt to the touch. The treatment for this type of burn is like the first degree, but healing might take longer. You might even have to take pain medicine to deal with the pain.

A fourth-degree burn, however, is the most severe of burns. These burns can destroy all layers of the skin, as well as bones, muscles, and tendons. A person who has suffered a fourth-degree burn will have to seek out medical help. If left untreated, these burns can be life-threatening. Treatment for these types of burns can be painful, long, and may even require invasive surgery.

Physical injuries come in all shapes, sizes, and severity. The treatment needed for those injuries will depend on the type of injury. Treatment could be immediate, or it could take a long time, and can even leave scars.

Sometimes we treat our physical injuries different than our invisible injuries. See, people who have been victimized in the past, may have healed from their physical injuries. But what happens to the verbal, emotional, and psychological damage? Those also need to be addressed. Those also need to be healed. And depending on the severity of the damage, the healing may be quick, or it could take a very long time.

Children (and some adults) are terrified of the doctor. Taking my kids to the doctor is not something I look forward to. No matter how much I explain and bribe them, the visits will always end in anxiety and tears. But as their mother, I know that if they are hurting, a visit to the doctor is in order.

Have you considered whether there are areas in your life where you might need help? Maybe you, like me, have been a Christian for a long time. Yet, there are still situations in your life that you struggle with. Maybe there are still scars that don't seem to heal, no matter what home remedies you have tried. A visit to the doctor may be in order.

The treatment might be quick and easy. However, it might also be painful and extensive. But treatment is necessary to achieve healing.

At your last doctors visit, do you remember having to fill out a form with your health history? You have to answer all types of questions about any illnesses, injuries, surgeries, allergies, and whether you are currently taking any medications. This form will help the doctor to understand you and assist you better.

Think of this book as that form. I encourage you to take your time reading, analyzing, meditating, and taking notes. There are some questions at the end of each chapter that have the purpose to help you in your journey of discovering those areas where you might need help.

CHAPTER 1

REJECTION CAN BE YOUR REDIRECTION

Tears streamed down my face as I confessed to the therapist that my marriage was falling apart. I blurted out that I felt worthless and useless because I couldn't be the wife that my husband deserved. Shame and guilt engulfed me because at almost forty years old, I still felt like that eight-year-old who had been told time and time again that she was worthless.

It wasn't that my life was terrible. It wasn't. I had a husband who loved me and told me so, constantly. I had two wonderful kids who were the light of my life. I also had the career that I had always dreamed of. Yet, those feelings of rejection and low self-esteem would often rear their ugly heads.

I have always been a reserved person. I don't share much of what's going on in my life. Sharing my feelings, thoughts, and struggles is not something that comes easy to me. Maybe that's why, externally, my life seemed perfect. Under all the façade, however, lurked feelings of rejection and a lack of self-worth.

I grew up with the notion that I was not important. I was raised by a male figure who seemed to relish in causing me pain. He constantly reminded me that my "real" father never wanted me. "When was the last time he got you a Christmas present?" he would ask me. My seven-year-old self couldn't answer, and he would say, "You, see? He doesn't love you; he doesn't care."

I knew he was right. My biological father was absent. My parents divorced before I was born, and he was never interested in having a relationship with me.

My mother sent me away when I was eleven years old to live with relatives. As an adult, I realized that this was eventually one of the best things that happened to me. It took me out of an abusive household. But at eleven, I didn't see it that way. I just knew I had been sent away. Unfortunately, my new home wasn't all that great. My relatives had many problems, and eventually, I took the brunt of their problems.

I have never been very confident—not in my abilities or looks, much less in my value as a person. I don't say this to invoke pity. I say this as a matter of fact. It's how I grew up feeling.

Ever since I was a young girl, I absorbed everything said about me. I absorbed everything that was done to me. Little by little, all those hateful and harsh words started forming invisible wounds in me. And those wounds became my constant companions. They became those pesky little visitors that could never find their way out. Sometimes at the slightest touch, the wounds would reopen.

Have you ever met someone who seemed to have it all together at first glance: a great family, a nice job, and a decent financial status, yet later you discover they hid a deep secret?

Maybe you are that person.

It seems like you have it all together. Your social media screams of success. Yet, no one knows of your deep invisible wounds.

This was also the story of Naaman in 2 Kings 5. Naaman was a well-regarded military commander. He was a respected and revered man in his circle. Yet, under all his uniform regalia and his position's distinction, he hid the fact that he was a leper.

Leprosy is a terrible disease for which there was no cure. It typically starts at the body's extremities, such as the toes or fingertips. It destroys the nerve cells, and the body tissue swells and gradually rots away. Being a leper in the past constituted a death sentence. You were destined to eventually die from the disease that little by little rotted your body, but you were also literally seen as an outcast. It was believed that leprosy was contagious, and nobody dared to touch a man ridden with the disease.

Yet Naaman was a military commander. From the outside, he lived the perfect life. But deep inside, he was suffering a slow death.

Many external factors contribute to a person's self-worth and self-esteem. Some of the most common factors are:

- What people say about you.
- What people have done to you.
- Your achievements or lack thereof.
- If you were looked down on.
- If you suffered a lack of love or affection.
- If you suffered some type of abuse.
- If you were forced to do something against your will.
- If you have been ignored.
- If others have been chosen over you.
- If you have been abandoned or cheated on.
- If you were an unplanned child.
- If your parents wanted a different gender.
- Etc.

Our experiences typically mold us into who we are—who we become. Pastor Tony Evans calls these experiences "tools of destiny".[1]

In his book *Detours,* he talks about these tools: The good, the bad, and the bitter.

> *The good are positive things that have happened as a result of God's will and your good choices. The bad are typically experiences such as*

mistakes, sins, failures, consequences, and regrets that have occurred because of your own choices. Bitter experiences are things that have happened to you but that are not your fault, such as abandonment, abuse, neglect, injustice, and disease.

In this book, we will be talking about the Bitter experiences. Not only will we talk about these experiences, but we will also learn who God says we are and how we can learn to see ourselves through His eyes.

Truth 1

Even through THE BITTER experiences,
God has a plan for you.

CHALLENGE 1

Think of experiences or situations in your life that can fall under the category of *bitter* experiences. Write those things down here:

_____

_____

_____

_____

What determines your self-worth? Is it what people say about you? Write down some examples:

_____

_____

_____

_____

Have you ever felt like you don't matter? Share more:

_____

_____

_____

_____

_____

Have you grown up believing all the labels that people attached to you? What are some of those labels?

_____

_____

_____

_____

_____

Have you adapted and adopted all those things people said about you that became a part of your identity? Explain how:

_____

_____

_____

_____

_____

_____

_____

_____

_____

_____

_____

CHAPTER 2

THROUGH THEIR EYES—STICKS AND STONES WILL BREAK MY BONES, BUT WORDS WILL HURT MY HEART

I decided to confide my deepest, darkest secret in a relative during my late teenage years. I shared with her about those terrible nights when I was awakened by the monster who, little by little, night after night, took my innocence. I shared with her all the horrible things he did and those he said to me. As the words poured out of my mouth, I felt a huge weight lift off my shoulders. The secret was no longer mine, I naively thought. I would finally be able to understand and heal from everything that had happened to me.

Unfortunately, healing was not what I received. As soon as the weight of my secret fell off my shoulders, a new chain locked itself across my heart. My relative told me that girls like me end up either being a prostitute or a lesbian.

I figured she was right.

What man would want to love someone who was broken? I accepted her words as truth because I honestly didn't think there was anything good in my future.

The physical injuries from the abuse had long since disappeared. Nonetheless, as I shared my story, new invisible wounds appeared.

Words have power

Think back to when God created the heavens and the earth. Genesis 1:3 says, "Then God said, 'Let there be light', and there was light". Verse 26 says, "Then God said, 'Let us make human beings in our image, to be like us' […]." With His words alone, God created something out of nothing. And not just any mundane thing; He even created man!

Have you ever stopped to consider that our words have the power of life and death? We have all heard the familiar saying "sticks and stones will break my bones, but words will never hurt me."

This is probably a response that has been uttered by many in the wake of name-calling or verbal bullying. Children in schools and playgrounds use this phrase as a repellent towards those who are likely bigger and stronger. More likely than not, however, those words play repeatedly in those children's minds. Because it is fair to say that *words indeed hurt.*

14

The Bible says in James 3:9-11, "With the tongue we praise our Lord and Father, and with it we curse human beings, who have been made in God's likeness. Out of the same mouth come praise and cursing. My brothers and sisters, this should not be. Can both fresh water and saltwater flow from the same spring?"

The words that come out of people's mouths can either be fruit or poison for our lives. Even well-intentioned people can say things that are derogatory to our identity and purpose. Many times, we build our confidence and our worth from the words and opinions of other people.

Life turns miserable when we allow the thoughts and opinions of others to define us. We become puppets of their sentiments and slaves of their perception. People say things to deflate our sense of worth and ridicule our sincere attempt to rise. They quickly remind us of our failures and hurl our mistakes at us. This can strongly influence how we see ourselves.

Especially now with the power of social media.

Social media is a powerful tool. It allows you to connect with family, friends, opportunities, services, and communities you may not otherwise have had access to. However, many studies have found that social media use is linked to anxiety, loneliness, and a feeling of low self-worth. According to some studies, social media use does appear to cause a decrease in self-esteem, with the age group most affected being girls between the ages of 10 and 14.[2]

In the world of social media, we allow anyone to criticize our lives by us making a post or uploading a picture or video. We willingly put ourselves on display so that people can throw their darts at us.

We have given people so much power.

We believe what other people say about us. Interestingly, we believe the negative others say about us more than the positive things.

Did you know that many people find it difficult to accept compliments? It could be because the person isn't sure the complimenter is sincere. Some people assume the complimenter is looking for something in return. Others don't believe they are worthy of the compliment. In the case of an insult or criticism it's different. We hardly hesitate to believe those.

I want to make a note and differentiate regular criticism from constructive criticism.

Constructive criticism provides a feedback that acknowledges both, the positives and where there is room for improvement instead of solely focusing on the negatives.

We agree that words can either be fruit or poison in our lives. We also agree that people's words can significantly affect our identity and self-worth.

But, have you considered how *your* words affect those around you? What kind of words pour out of *your* mouth? When your children do something that you dislike, what is the first thing that comes rushing out of your mouth? When your husband "forgets" to place his dirty clothes in the hamper, do you rudely remind him that clearly his mother didn't do a good job raising him?

I have always been very intentional about the words that I use for my children. Speaking with kindness and grace does not come naturally to me. Unconsciously, we raise our children how we were raised. If we were raised in a household where yelling, criticism, and condemnation was the norm, that is probably what will come out of our mouth. Therefore, we must be intentional, mindful, and actively cognizant of the words that come out of our mouths.

Children are like sponges. They absorb everything. It should be our goal to make sure we are speaking words of life into their lives.

Our words do more than just convey information, they have the power to impact the people around us. Out of all the creatures on this planet, only humans can communicate through spoken words. Let's choose to use this unique and powerful gift given by God to positively impact those around us.

A man has joy by the answer of his mouth, and a word spoken in due season, how good it is!

PROVERBS 15:23 (NKJV)

17

Truth 2

Words can either be fruit or poison.

CHALLENGE 2

When someone says something about you, ask yourself these questions:

- Is what the person saying true?
- Is the person saying it out of love?
- Is there anything I can do to change?

Think of those closest to you (i.e., spouse, children, parents, co-workers). List the words that you have used in the past or currently use with these people.

Fruit   Poison

_____   _____

_____   _____

_____   _____

_____   _____

_____   _____

_____   _____

_____   _____

_____   _____

_____   _____

_____   _____

CHAPTER 3

THROUGH YOUR EYES—MIRROR; MIRROR ON THE WALL, WHO'S THE FAIREST OF THEM ALL

As soon as I felt the scissors, I knew I had made a mistake. I should not have gone to get a haircut. I wanted a short bob like the styles I had seen in a style magazine. Instead, I looked like I was wearing a helmet on my head.

I came back home, hoping no one would notice. As soon as I entered the house, he saw me. He took one look at my hair and blurted out, "What in the world did you do to your hair? You look so ugly!" I quickly ran into my room while tears streamed down my face. I knew I looked ugly. But this confirmation made it a thousand times worse.

If you had to describe yourself with one word, what would that be?

Many times, it's easier for people to use positive and endearing adjectives to describe another person than it is to describe themselves, especially if we have grown up hearing negative things about ourselves.

In Exodus 3:8, God promised Moses that His people would inherit the land that flowed with milk and honey.

But there was a caveat.

The people would first have to go into the land and defeat the people that lived there. Moses sent spies to go ahead of them and inspect the land. Joshua and Caleb were among the spies. When the men returned, they reported what they had seen and heard. The men confirmed that the land did, in fact, flow with milk and honey. It was precisely what God had promised!

But there was a problem, according to the men. Yes, the land flows with milk and honey, they said. However, there are also giants in that land, in addition to milk and honey. In comparison to them, the men said we *seemed* like grasshoppers in *our* own eyes. And we are pretty sure, they determined, that is precisely how they see us.

It's interesting to see how these men confirmed God's promise to them. The land did flow with milk and honey! It was exactly what God had said it was.

But they also saw the giants.

The Bible *doesn't* say that the giants saw them and called them grasshoppers. It was *them* who compared themselves to the giants and automatically disqualified themselves!

They saw *themselves* as grasshoppers.

They decided in their minds that the physical height of the men was enough to defeat them. But it didn't only stop there. They assumed that the giants saw them that way as well. "[A]nd we looked the same to them […]."

Has God ever promised something to you? It was a promise so close that you could smell it, taste it, and see it. But you also saw the giant. You saw the giant and immediately disqualified yourself. You figured that there was no way you could defeat that giant. In comparison, you are only a tiny grasshopper.

One of the Bible stories above other stories that broke my heart is this one. The Israelites were so close to the promise. They could taste it. But their fear was more substantial. Fear won. Of the original 600 adult males, plus adult women: none other than Joshua, Caleb, and their families, entered the promised land.

God has made promises to each one of us. Some of those promises are so close to being fulfilled. But we must take a step of faith. While we need to believe in the promise, we also have to act.

God promised the Israelites that He would be with them. He would give them the strength to defeat the giants. God knew there were giants in the promised land. But He also knew that with His help, the Israelites would defeat them. Unfortunately, the Israelites only believed half of the promise. They were too afraid to trust that God would help them defeat the giants. Because they saw the size of the giants with their physical eyes, they saw themselves as insignificant grasshoppers. And they

figured there was no way that they could defeat them—
what a sad story.

Sometimes, promises come with conditions. And the
conditions can come in the form of defeating giants. But
along with the promise and conditions, comes the
certainty that God will help you defeat those giants. Yes,
they may be taller, stronger, and scarier. But you have in
you the One who created the heavens and the earth.
Don't let self-doubt keep you from achieving all the
promises that God has in store for you.

It may well be that when you look at yourself in the
mirror, you see someone who is not strong enough. Or
someone who is not worthy enough. You fill in the
blanks. You are seeing yourself through your physical
eyes. It's time we look at ourselves through *His* eyes.

Truth 3

Past experiences may have distorted our perception of ourselves.

CHALLENGE 3

- When you see yourself in the mirror, what do you
  see?

_____

_____

_____

_____

_____

- Write down three words that you typically use to
  describe yourself:

_____

_____

_____

_____

_____

- Are you willing to believe God's promises for your
  life and see yourself through His eyes?

_____

_____

_____

_____

_____

CHAPTER 4

IT'S NOT ALL ABOUT YOU

My daughter was four years old when my son— her little brother—was born. During the first four years of her life she was the center of attention. She was spoiled by us and by her grandparents. Things changed when my son was born. Now my daughter had to share all that attention.

Debbie has always been a pleasant and easy going child but there were times during my son's first year where she pouted and cried when she felt she wasn't getting enough attention. She would often ask, *why does he get to do that and I can't?* I would then sit down and explain to her that we did do all those things with her when she was younger.

According to Jean Piaget, a famous Swiss psychologist known for his work on child development, children below the age of two years old think that the universe revolves around them.[3] So much so, that they believe objects and people only exist for as long as they are staring at them. It's only after the age of two that they begin to recognize this is not the case.

Unfortunately, some of us continue to think we are the center of the universe. This idea can manifest in different ways in our lives. One of those ways is taking offense to everything that happens or is done to us. This would happen to me when my husband came home and was grouchy or showed an unpleasant attitude toward me. My first thought was always, *what did I do wrong? There must be something wrong with* me.

Something that has helped me in this journey is starting with the premise that people are not coming from a bad place.

So, I start from the premise that my husband is not coming from a bad place, that there must be a reason behind his attitude—and more than likely, that reason has nothing to do with me. It could be that he had a bad day at work. Maybe traffic was worse than usual. The maybes can go on and on.

In the previous chapters, I discussed how our past experiences influence us to see ourselves differently. Yes, we are all subject to malicious people who want to harm us. While others may be well-intentioned, their words can still negatively impact us. But I believe it is safe to say that the majority of events going on around us have nothing to do with us.

The second way this concept can manifest in our lives is when many of us believe we are entitled to everything. Entitlement culture is so prevalent in our current society. We are encouraged to behave as if we deserve to have things given to us. This culture encourages the idea that we merit special treatment and privileges. Some of us go as far as thinking that society and the world around us "owe" us something. And when we don't get what we think we deserve, we punish, resent, or blame anyone that stands in our way.

It's important to understand that there is a difference between rights and entitlement. For example, as American citizens we have certain rights granted to us by the Constitution of the United States—for example, life, liberty, and the pursuit of happiness.

The issue with entitlement is that we believe we are exempt from responsibility and that we are owed special treatments when nothing has been done to earn it. Perhaps the things we have gone through in the past account for this perception. We believe that our past suffering makes us entitled to compensation in the present. That can certainly be the case in some circumstances. If we have been wronged in some way, we can certainly seek justice. For example, there are certain laws that provide that if you have been injured in some way, you may be entitled to monetary compensation.

But we cannot live our entire lives thinking we are entitled to everything we want. We cannot live our lives thinking the universe revolves around us. It doesn't. The sooner we realize this, the sooner we will be able to start taking responsibility for our own actions. We can't undo what was done to us in the past, but we can certainly control how we respond and react in the present.

Don't get me wrong. You are special. After all, God made you! You are His special treasure. But the world does not revolve around us.

The world does not revolve around me.

I had to learn this truth, because I used to take people's silence, attitudes, and actions as a direct attack. The reality is that most people are so caught up in their own lives that they don't care about what you do. People have their struggles, their concerns, and their problems. People pay less attention to us than we think.

It's important to realize that something which bothers you might not bother someone else. If someone upset you unintentionally, they won't know until you tell them! We can't keep expecting people to magically know what is on our minds because, more than likely, they have other things to worry about.

Instead of taking everything that happens around me personally, I have learned to recognize that most events are beyond my control and have little to do with me.

There's an old proverb that says, "Seek to understand before seeking to be understood."

- The text you're not getting a reply to? It's not necessarily about what you wrote, but what the recipient is going through.
- The sale that didn't go through? It doesn't necessarily have to do with your capabilities, but instead with what is going on with everybody else.

- The harsh word that just cut through your heart? It's not necessarily about your relationship or interaction with the other person, but instead, about some difficult battle they're fighting elsewhere.
- The kind word that goes unnoticed. It's not about them being ungrateful, but about what else is going on in the world.
- The person who didn't wave back? It's not about them ignoring you, maybe they were not wearing their glasses and didn't see you.
- The job you didn't get? Maybe the person they hired was the most qualified.
- The person that cut you off in traffic?...

Truth 4

It's not all about you.

CHALLENGE 4

Are you willing to extend mercy to others?

_____

_____

_____

_____

_____

_____

_____

_____

Think of a situation when you judged someone without knowing what was going on in their lives. What might you do differently in that situation?

_____

_____

_____

_____

_____

_____

_____

_____

_____

CHAPTER 5

PAINFULLY VISIBLE AND ENTIRELY IGNORED

I have always been afraid of trying out new things. All through my time at university, I kept feeling like I was not smart enough.

In school, there is a specific type of students known as *gunners*. Gunners always have the answers—or at least they pretend they do. They are the ones that raise their hand before the professor even finishes asking the questions. Gunners intimidated me. I could' understand how they were able conclude so quickly when I could not even understand what the professor was talking about.

It was unusual for me to volunteer an answer. I only

answered if I was sure I had the correct answer.

As I looked around at my classmates, I thought everyone was more intelligent than me. I didn't think I belonged. I almost disqualified myself before anyone else did.

The way we value and see ourselves affects every area of our lives. I once heard someone say that you are exactly what you think you should be right now.

Have you ever lost an opportunity because you disqualified yourself? Many people don't even try because they already know they won't get picked, so why even try?

COVID-19 has changed all our lives. This pandemic has completely transformed the way we live. Incredibly, this virus affected the United States as well as the rest of the world. One of the most devastating outcomes that the virus brought was the loss of jobs for thousands of people. Now, losing a job is a bad thing, but the number of people that lost their job at once during the pandemic was highly devastating.

With the loss of jobs came this term, which is not new but came along with the pandemic and acquired a life of its own: *non-essential*.

What does it mean to be non-essential in times of COVID? It means that you are not as important as another person and that your positions can be eliminated. The product or services you offer are not as important as a business. People can live without it or survive without it for some time. It's hard to imagine what it would be like to one day arrive at work and find out that you are no longer needed because your services are not essential; they are not vital.

Of course, the term non-essential isn't new to this pandemic. But it's not a term that was used as often. However, other terms are synonymous that we use as part of our vocabulary, such as worthless, useless, and good for nothing.

How many times during our lifetime have we heard these words? Maybe not directly to our face, but implied? How often have you experienced a situation where your presence wasn't missed? When people didn't care whether you were there or not. What is worse, how many times did we deem *ourselves* non-essential? We disqualified ourselves before the race even started. We do this many times, often without even noticing.

All those invisible wounds led me to live a very guarded life. I have experienced rejection so much that my walls were constantly up. It's a self-protection mechanism. I wouldn't let people get too close because I knew that rejection was coming. And to avoid the rejection, I would just hold people at arm's length. Sadly, I have done this with people closest to me, including my husband.

One of my husband's love languages is words of affirmation. He tells me that he loves me and that I am beautiful more than 100 times a day. I am not exaggerating. But because my self-esteem and self-worth were practically nonexistent, I often heard his words but did not believe them. I figured he had to say those things because he was my husband. I felt he was obligated to say so. Like a mother saying her baby was cute even though he wasn't. She sees him with the eyes of a mother. I thought my husband didn't mean those things; he said them because he had to. Michelle, my therapist, once told me that not every husband tells his wife she's beautiful. If he's saying it, he must mean it.

Remember Naaman from Chapter 1? He went to a prophet to be healed. He figured he would be welcomed with pomp and circumstance that reflected the powerful man he was. Instead, the prophet sent a messenger who told Naaman to go and wash in the Jordan river seven times, so that he would be clean. It sounded simple enough, right? Too simple, thought Naaman. He was upset and offended that he was sent to do something so simple. He was expecting something grander. The bible says that he turned away in a rage.

Many times, we live with deeply hidden secrets. We hide our shame, lack of self-worth, and lack of confidence undercoats. God wants to heal us. And sometimes He will do it in the simplest ways. But we must be willing.

The officers traveling with Naaman said, "Sir, if the prophet had told you to do something very difficult, wouldn't you have done it? So, you should certainly obey him when he says simply, 'Go and wash and be cured!'" (2 Kings 5:13).

Obedience required that Naaman get down in the water and dip seven times. When he obeyed God, he was made whole. In fact, his skin was restored to a better condition than it was. According to the Bible, it was "like unto the flesh of a little child."

God wants to heal you. What is He asking you to do? True obedience to God requires us to take God at His word.

Trust in the Lord with all your heart and lean not on your own understanding; in all your ways acknowledge Him and He shall direct your paths. Do not be wise in your own eyes; fear the Lord and depart from evil. It will be health to your flesh, and strength to your bones.

PROVERBS 3:5-8 (NKJV)

Truth 5

We often disqualify ourselves.

CHALLENGE 5

Think of a situation where you disqualified yourself. Write about it here:

_____

_____

_____

_____

How might your life be different now if you hadn't disqualified yourself?

_____

_____

_____

_____

Is there something specific that God is asking you to do? What is it?

_____

_____

_____

_____

_____

CHAPTER 6

THE LITTLE ENGINE THAT COULD

I saw a video once that greatly touched my life. Although, I think the perspective I gathered from it was not the intended one. The video showed a group of kids lined up in a starting line to compete in a track race. However, only certain kids were allowed to start when the whistle blew. Some of the other kids were allowed to start after the others had gotten a head start. The group of kids who started first didn't face any obstacles on their path. However, the other kids had struggles with every couple of steps.

The first group of kids finished the race without much struggle. They didn't even seem tired. The other group didn't fare as well as the first group. Because of how easy the other ones had it; some kids in the second group quit. Others just stared in disbelief as the kids in the first group ran and reached their goal. However, some kids in the second group seemed upset at what was an unfair situation. But they gathered their strength, fought against the struggles, and crossed the finish line. They didn't win. If the race were timed, they indeed would have been disqualified. But they crossed the finish line, nonetheless.

The purpose of the video was to show the disparity between the two groups. Many who saw it were indignant that the second group had to struggle so much before the race started. Many excused those who quit, expressing that they didn't even have a chance and that the race was too unfair.

I did not see it that way. Yes, it was unfair. Ideally, all the kids should have started simultaneously, and either all had struggles or none. But what I focused on was that none of the kids in the second group were prevented from finishing the race. Yes, it took some of them much longer, and it was harder for them. But they were able to finish.

Sometimes it feels like life is not fair. Other people seem to have it easier than us.

We are not all called to do the same things, carry out the same tasks, or accomplish the same goals. But what is true is that we have all been called to something.

God has made each of us in His image and, as such, we are full of potential. Potential that was meant just for you.

Sometimes, we are afraid of failure because we don't consider ourselves capable of handling the task. To be honest, we may be right. It might be the case that we lack the required experience or skills. In that case, what can we do?

First, we must acknowledge that we are not capable at the moment. The second step is figuring out what to do about it, because we can disqualify ourselves, quit, or not even try. Or we can figure out what we need to do to become capable or skilled.

There are certain things in my life that could be considered as disadvantages—for example, I am an immigrant; English is my second language; I suffered abuse at a young age; I did not have wealthy parents; and the list could go on.

I am the type of person who needs to read something more than once to grasp it. In school, sometimes I felt overwhelmed. Our assignments consisted of reading hundreds of pages, some of which I did not understand. I was not one of those students who could read the material once and grasp it entirely. I had to take my time reading and likely read the material at least twice to understand it.

It took me approximately seven years to finish what should have been a four-year undergraduate degree. I was working full time because I had to pay my way. There were semesters when I could not afford a full load of classes. It would have been easy for me to quit and complain that I didn't have parents who could afford to put me through college. I didn't have parents who could help me go to school full time.

But my perspective was: I will be able to finish. Although it took me nearly twice as long, nobody stopped me.

What's your list? Are there things in your life that

could be viewed as disadvantages?

We must understand who we are and where we are coming from. We must understand our weaknesses and our strengths. I knew myself and knew that I had to put an extra effort on my studies to succeed. I would have to put in more time, hours, and energy. But I was willing to do it because I wanted to achieve my goal.

Many people are afraid to acknowledge their shortcomings and weaknesses. I believe that this is a mistake. By acknowledging them you can then know what you need to do to be successful, but successful in your path—not someone else's version of success. It may take you more work than what it takes others, but that is okay. Life is not a race where the first to make it wins it all.

Moses was tasked with one of the biggest jobs in history. The people of Israel had been enslaved in Egypt. God told Moses to go and talk to Pharaoh to let His people go. Moses immediately made excuses as to why this was not a good idea. But out of the many excuses that Moses gave God, the one that caught my attention was when Moses told God that he was not the right person to talk to Pharaoh because he was not eloquent.

Exodus 4:10 says, "Then Moses said to the Lord, 'O my Lord, I am not eloquent, neither before nor since You have spoken to Your servant, but I am slow of speech and slow of tongue.'"

Moses brought up the fact that he did not consider himself capable of achieving the task that had been assigned. Moses did not believe he was the right guy.

When I think of Moses, I remember that Moses wasn't just any old schmuck that God picked out of a lineup. Acts 7:22 states that Moses was learned in all the wisdom of the Egyptians and was mighty in words and deeds. This doesn't even sound like the same guy! How could a guy who was mighty in words claim not to be eloquent? Moses had been brought up in the palace. The likes of Pharaoh had surrounded him.

What was the real reason why Moses doubted his abilities? Was it the fact that it had been so long since he had to speak to the likes of Pharaoh that he had forgotten what it was like? Was his self-confidence gone because he had been surrounded mostly by sheep as of late? Whatever the reason was, Moses did not feel up to the task.

God, however, knew Moses' capability. He had been with Moses. When God asked Moses to talk to Pharaoh, he promised that He would be with Him. Did Moses doubt that God would keep His promise?

Many times, we lack confidence in our abilities. Maybe it has been such a long time since we have done something that we no longer feel capable of. Maybe we feel that we are too old. Too old to learn the language. Too old to learn a new task. Too old to dust off the old brain and remember or re-learn things. We are afraid that we won't measure up to the task. And like Moses, we excuse ourselves.

But God created us. He knows our weaknesses and our strengths. And He promises to be with us.

Exodus 4:11-12 says, "So the Lord said to him, 'who has made man's mouth? Or who makes the mute, the deaf, the seeing, or the blind? Have not I, the Lord? Therefore, go, and I will be with your mouth and teach you what you shall say.'"

I find so interesting that God is so specific in His words to Moses. He is not only telling him that He will be with Him. He tells him, I will be with your *mouth*. The specific thing that you think is useless. The thing that you think will stop you from carrying out the task.

"I will be with your mouth."

If Moses was not an eloquent speaker, God knew it, yet He chose him still. God did not make a mistake choosing Moses.

God did not make a mistake choosing you.

Truth 6

People are often afraid to admit their
shortcomings and weaknesses.

CHALLENGE 6

Are you willing to allow God to work through your weaknesses and inabilities?

_____

_____

_____

_____

Write down 3 things that you consider to be weaknesses in your life:

_____

_____

_____

_____

_____

Think of a specific goal that you want to achieve. What is that goal?

_____

_____

_____

_____

Are you currently qualified and prepared to carry out that goal? If yes, what has stopped you?

_____

_____

_____

_____

_____

If no, write down three steps that you can actively take to become qualified or get better prepared to achieve that goal:

_____

_____

_____

_____

_____

_____

_____

_____

_____

_____

CHAPTER 7

IF YOU CAN'T CHANGE YOUR SITUATION, CHANGE YOUR MIND

I was very excited about a talk that my university had organized. The guest speaker was a prominent judge. He is very famous, and you can tell he has done very well for himself. He is very accomplished, and I was very excited about the privilege of hearing him speak.

He was only about five minutes into his talk when he said to the entire room of predominantly minority students, "You are all victims. Society has mistreated you, and you are all victims."

I remember hearing his words and feeling as if a bucket of cold water had just been poured on my face. Yes, I agreed. I had been a victim of many things. But I refused to continue using the label as if it was a badge of honor. I WAS a victim. Had been in the past. But I no longer saw myself as one and took offense to anyone, especially a prominent, rich, famous person telling me I was. Because I had decided that if I wanted to succeed in life and experience all that God had for me, I needed to start seeing myself from a different perspective.

The previous chapters have mostly been about how people's words and actions affect us and how our self-worth is molded because of those words. Words that we take hold of and believe. Now comes the hard part.

Because now we are at a crossroads.

For many years I lived thinking that not only was I worthless, but I was a victim. And as a victim, I could live under the banner of victimhood for the rest of my life. One day, however, after I saw myself through the eyes of God, I realized that, in fact, yes, I *had* been a victim. I had suffered abuse. I had been called useless, dumb, worthless, and good for nothing.

But that's not who I was anymore.

I had to choose. I could either continue to live as I was or change my identity and begin a new life. As a survivor, as worthy, capable and confident. It would not be easy, as I would have to accept responsibility for my thoughts and actions. I would be held responsible for the choices that I made.

That is the difference between a victim and a victor.

> Victors take a proactive approach to life. They don't believe they are confined to their current position, choosing instead to continuously seek ways to improve their

situation. Victors just want to know what the opportunity is. They don't need to be convinced, cajoled, or coaxed to perform.

Victims believe that life happens to them and there is nothing they can do to change it. They believe that someone else can and should improve their lot in life, and they demand that those around them should make them happy. They spend their lives in fear about what will come next. Victims are just trying to survive in life and have their focus squarely on themselves.[4]

So, how do you go from a victimhood mentality to a victor mentality? How do you learn to see yourself in a different light? When you have lived all your life thinking that you are worthless, how do you change your perspective?

Romans 12:2 is an excellent place to start. The New Living Translation version states, "Don't copy the behavior and customs of this world, but let God transform you into a new person by *changing the way you think.* Then you will learn God's will for you, which is good and pleasing and perfect."

The King James Version states, "And be not conformed to this world: but be ye transformed by the renewing of your mind that ye may prove what is that good, and acceptable, and perfect, will of God."

God is such a loving Father. He knows that we must change how we think, value, and see ourselves. Because once our minds are renewed, with God's help, we can start seeing ourselves with His eyes and realize that we are:

- A child of God (John 1:12)
- Completely forgiven (Colossians 1:14)
- Tenderly loved by God (Jeremiah 31:3)
- The sweet fragrance of Christ to God (2 Corinthians 2:15)
- Christ's friend (John 15:15)
- Chosen by God, holy and dearly loved (Colossians 3:12)
- God's workmanship (Ephesians 2:10)

Where do you stand today? Are you ready to step out of your comfort zone? Are you ready to step out of a victimhood mentality? Are you ready to start the journey of renewing your mind?

It's not an easy task, but it is entirely worth it. If you are ready, there are specific steps that you will need to take.

1. Renew Your Mind

Pastor Craig Groeschel says in his book *Winning the War in Your Mind,* "[y]our life is always moving in the direction of your strongest thoughts."[5] So, what are your strongest thoughts? Satan's most common attacks against the minds of Christians are some of the followings:

- I am unworthy
- I am unloved
- I am incapable
- I am undesirable
- I am unforgivable
- I am incompetent
- I am unknown

- My life is insignificant
- I am a mistake
- I am not essential

But once we start seeing ourselves through God's eyes, we can start renewing our minds and changing our thoughts.

In her bible study book, *The Armor of God,* Priscilla Shirer gives four steps that serve as a defense against the enemy's attempts to infiltrate our minds:[6]

1. Step 1: *Identify* the toxic thought patterns you've been nursing and recognize them for what they truly are- strongholds that, along with the enemy, you've assisted in constructing in your mind.

2. Step 2: *Confess* errant thought processes to God and agree with Him about your responsibility in helping to construct these strongholds in your life. Our strongholds are not all the enemy's fault. Every time we nurse and rehearse illegitimate thinking; we add another concrete brick to the construction of a stronghold. Whether those thoughts are in relation to doubt, fear, insecurity, salacious imaginations, or something else entirely, rehearsing the enemy's lies makes us in essence a partner with the enemy in building up a fortress that holds us captive.

3. Step 3: *Dismantle* the stronghold by taking your thoughts captive, then renewing your perspective and understanding through the concentrated and deliberate application of God's truth.

The act of *renewing our minds* is not a one-time event. It's not like taking a pill for a headache. It is a lifestyle. It is taking a proactive approach to our daily life.

The most practical way to start the process of renewing our minds is by going to the source—the Bible. In the Bible we discover what God says about us, what He thinks about us, and the promises He has made to us.

I am sure that if you are reading this book, you should have access to a Bible. I have many versions of the Bible in my house, and I also carry it on my phone as an app. I am positive you do as well. We can have the Bible around us, but it is not enough just to carry it around and read a verse or two now and then.

If we want to renew our minds and take an active approach, we must do more. Here are some active examples:

- Find verses that speak to your weakness
- Meditate on those verses
- Memorize the verses

And now, dear brothers and sisters, one final thing. Fix your thoughts on what is true, honorable, right, pure, lovely, and admirable. Think about things that are excellent and worthy of praise.

PHILIPPIANS 4:8 (NLT)

---

2. Set Boundaries

Setting up boundaries is an essential step to realizing your worth. It is vital to take an honest look at those who surround you. We have many circles of people around us. Some we choose, and others choose us. But as adults, we have the power whether or not to keep people close to us. This is not an easy task, but it must be done.

Have you noticed that certain people make you a better person? You enjoy talking to them because they lift you (your spirit); they share in your struggles and your victories. It is as if your battery is recharged every time you are with them.

I have experienced butterflies in my stomach. Although to me, they are more like a swarm of bees. This happens to me every time I come across certain people. It's people who drain me not only physically but mentally. Their presence in my life doesn't cause peace. Many times, I feel physically drained after being around such people.

Many of us have learned that it is important to be kind and helpful. This is what I believe. Nonetheless, when you recognize that someone is not helping you, you need to set boundaries and remove them from your life. I believe this has two purposes. First, it shows you that you can choose the type of people close to you. The second purpose of this action is to show those people that you won't tolerate their behavior.

I have two young kids. Kids are extremely smart, and they'll push you to see how far you will let them go. The more they push, the more they try. And the more you give in, the more they will push. Sometimes it is the same with adults. Some people in your life will speak to you in a certain way. If you don't stop them and tell them that it is unacceptable, they will keep doing it. And sometimes we don't do it because we are trying to be polite. I get it. But it's important to set boundaries.

In his book *Boundaries*, Dr. Henry Cloud explains: [7]

> Boundaries define us. They define what is me and what is not me. A boundary shows me where I end and where someone else begins, leading me to a sense of ownership.

> Boundaries help us distinguish our property so that we can take care of it. They help us to "guard our heart with all diligence." We need to keep things that will nurture us inside our fences and keep things that will harm us outside. In short, boundaries help us keep the good in and the bad out.

What words are you allowing people to call you? What labels are you allowing people to stick on you?

Allow. That is a strong word. Because now you have the power of God to remove yourself from people and situations that bring down your spirit rather than building it up. "It isn't going to be easy," I said. It may just be that you need to let go of some people in your life. Even family members. Ouch. Are you not ready to let them go? You can distance yourself.

Proverbs 22:3 says that "The prudent man sees the evil and hides himself."

We often allow people to speak words of death and fear into our lives. But we think we have to put up with it. You don't. God is your maker. He made you according to His image. He is your mirror.

When was the last time you stood up firm to someone who tried to push you down? God has not given us a spirit of fear but of love and a sound mind.

What are you believing? Do you accept a compliment and believe it? Sometimes we have to train our minds to accept positive things that are being said about ourselves. It is easy to accept the negative things and dismiss the positive things.

It is easy to dismiss the music we listen to and the shows we watch as pure entertainment. But all these things are feeding something into our spirit. Are they feeding things that encourage you and build up your worth and value, or are they subconsciously tearing you down?

3. Choose to Forgive

A lot of who we are is caused by some bitter things that Tony Evans explains in his book. Things that we had no control over. But there comes a season in our lives where we must take full responsibility for our actions. That is the difference between a victim and a victor. A victor makes a choice and takes responsibility for the outcome. A victim blames everyone else and assumes that he has no choice.

Forgiveness is one of those actions. I have heard the saying many times that forgiveness is not a feeling; it is an action that we must take. Because we often won't feel like forgiving—maybe we never will. But if we *decide* to forgive, we can move on with our lives.

Many people are hesitant to forgive because they

have the mistaken belief that forgiveness means letting the person who hurt you off the hook. But forgiveness is not the same as justice, nor does it require reconciliation. Forgiveness is letting go of sin. It is moving on instead of dwelling on that sin and harboring it against the person who hurt us.

Forgiveness does not come easy. It didn't come easy to me. For a long time, I held a grudge against those who I thought were supposed to protect me when I was a child. It really wasn't until I learned of the implications that the lack of forgiveness would have on my life, that I made the conscious decision to forgive.

The lack of forgiveness affects not only our mental health, but our physical and spiritual health as well. There are studies that show the correlation between lack of forgiveness and anxiety, depression, and even heart diseases.[8]

Most importantly, in my opinion, is what the lack of forgiveness does to our relationship with God. The forgiveness that we receive from God is tied to our forgiving others. When we forgive, we are allowing God to have more influence and power in our lives.

Resentment is like drinking poison and waiting for the other person to die.

ST. AUGUSTINE

Do you have bitterness in your heart and a grudge against the person or incident that hurt you so badly? Have you not forgiven that person? This lack of forgiveness can hold you down too long in the chute of mediocrity. If you hold these grudges in, you are limiting the life and grace offered by God.

God has forgiven us.

Then Peter came to him and asked, 'Lord, how often should I forgive someone who sins against me? Seven times?' 'No, not seven times.' Jesus replied, 'but seventy times seven!'

MATTHEW 18:21-22 (NLT)

---

4. Seek Out Wise Counsel

For many years I suffered in silence. Fear, embarrassment, guilt, and lack of direction led me to encapsulate my suffering. I know I am not the only one this happens to. Many of us suffer in silence because we are afraid.

But we are not meant to walk this journey alone. God, in his love and mercy, has also equipped people and has given each one of us different skills, gifts, and ways to help each other. Pastors, professional counselors, friends, and ministries are all different examples of people that God can use to help us heal.

• The Holy Spirit

For three years the disciples walked alongside Jesus. They had the immense honor of witnessing the life of the

Messiah and living life with Him by their side. So, it's understandable that when Jesus explained that He would soon be leaving them, the disciples were afraid.

Jesus understood their fears and explained to them that He would ask the Father to send an Advocate who would never leave them—The Holy Spirit. This advocate would be there to lead and guide them.

That same promise that Jesus made to His disciples also applies to us. The Holy Spirit is our helper and is here to walk alongside our most difficult journeys.

- Professional Counselors

Many Christians have always been hesitant when it comes to seeking help from professional counselors such as therapists, psychologists, and counselors.

Joy Dyer from The Potter's House Ministries states that "while it's not taboo within Christian circles to see a doctor for a physical ailment, an extended hesitation precedes seeing a counselor for a mental ailment. In both cases, the helping party is a trained professional dedicated to your well-being, so what's the hang up?

For one, we may feel guilt admitting we need help outside of leaning on our faith, our relationship with God, and our church community. Somehow, seeking therapy has subconsciously been correlated to a lack of faith or a "weak prayer life." But this kind of thinking that reduces mental health to spiritual deficiencies is neither productive nor biblically sound. Proverbs 15:22 (NASB) tells, "Without consultation, plans are frustrated, but with many counselors they succeed."

With the help of a professional counselor, I was able to overcome many of the barriers that were still holding me back and were not allowing me to live a full life. My therapist is a God-fearing woman who not only prayed with me, but taught me tools and gave me resources to be able to deal with those wounds that were still affecting my life.

- Pastors and Church Community

I am very blessed to have pastors who have prayed for me and guided me with tools to experience inner healing. Some people believe that when you accept Jesus in your heart, all your problems are immediately solved. Addictions, hang-ups, wounds, bitterness, all go away. Although this may be true for some, it is likely not reality for the majority.

The Christian life is a constant daily walk. Every day we must make choices that will help us either grow, heal, and mature. Some churches are very good about not only preaching about the redeeming work of Christ, but also in providing resources such as workshops, trainings, counseling services, retreats, and many other tools that can help us become the person God intended for us to be.

All of you together are Christ's body, and each of you is a part of it. Here are some parts God has appointed for the church: first are the apostles, second are prophets, third are teachers, then those who do miracles, those who have the gift of healing, those who can help others, those who have the gift of leadership, those who speak in unknown languages.

1 CORINTHIANS 12:27-28 (NLT)

Truth 7

We have all been victims of something but
through Christ we can find a path to victory.

CHALLENGE 7

Are you willing to dispose of the banner of victimhood and actively work to walk in victory?

_____

_____

_____

_____

Write down 3 practical steps to make this happen:

_____

_____

_____

_____

_____

What are some practical steps you can take towards your path of healing?

_____

_____

_____

_____

_____

CHAPTER 8

THROUGH HIS EYES–
I WILL BE WITH YOU

Years ago, I received a word that I truly believe came from God.

We were at a conference, and a prophet of God spoke to me and said the following:

> Barbara, I see you as a flower in His garden. There was a time when there were curses spoken against you. You felt that you were less than usable. You thought, *how could the Lord even use me?* But the Lord says, Barbara, I have clipped you from the outside garden, and I have planted you in the inner court. That inner

court to where He can be intimate with you, and He can reveal that father's love that you have never known. You had not known an earthly father's love and a love that was not of the Lord.

He is taking His hands and arms and wrapping them around you. He is placing that hand of assurance to assure you, for He has called you. There is a calling in your life, and He has not passed you by. He has transplanted you from the outer court into the inner court that He may brood over you, and He might attend to all your needs.

This word is a treasured memory of mine. I often return to it when I feel my wounds opening back up. It is not just me who these words are for. I encourage you today to make those words your own. Be assured that God sees you. He will have you transplanted to the inner courts. He will be with you and take care of all your needs.

The Bible says in Ephesians 2:10 that we are His workmanship, His handiwork. Have you ever sat down to consider this?

I believed I was worthless, useless, and good for nothing. I believed that God must have made a mistake with me. I was abused and used, which made me a pretty broken mess. But God used the bitter things to make a beautiful thing out of my life. God made me with a purpose. The things that I went through as a child were painful, and I wouldn't wish them on anyone. But God has used those things for good. Once I decided to have faith in God's creation and His workmanship, I realized that I am who He needs me to be.

The Devil knows how you are, but if you let him, he will make you think and focus on the worst of how you are. And the Devil is also a master deceiver. In this journey, we need to constantly remind ourselves of who made us and that there is a purpose in the way we are. Because if we are not careful, our insecurities can lead us to make wrong decisions.

This is what happened to Eve in the garden. God told Adam and Eve that they could eat from any tree in the garden, except for one. The serpent then asked Eve if God had told them that they couldn't eat from any trees. By doing this, the serpent planted a seed of insecurity in Eve. Eve then felt as if she was being left out. Like there was something God didn't want to share with her. Her insecurity then led her to make the wrong decision, which led them to disobey.

In earlier chapters, I discussed the various things that affects our values, self-esteem, and how we see ourselves. But where should our value come from? Let's read the following verses and see what value we have in God's eyes:

• We are valuable because we were made in the image of God.

  –So, God created human beings in his image. In the image of God, he created them; male and female, he created them. (Genesis 1:27)

• We are valuable because God said it. He called us His unique treasure.

–Now, if you obey me and keep my covenant, you will be my unique treasure from among all the peoples on earth. (Exodus 19:5)

• We are valuable because God paid a high price for us.

–For this is how God loved the world: He gave his one and only Son so that everyone who believes in him will not perish but have eternal life. (John 3:16)

• We are valuable because God is with us.

–We now have this light shining in our hearts, but we are like fragile clay jars containing this great treasure. This clarifies that our great power is from God, not from ourselves. (2 Corinthians 4:7)

According to Dr. Ben E. Benjamin, a hundred years ago, about 99% of babies in orphanages in the United States died before they were seven months old. These orphanages provided the babies with what they deemed were the essentials—roof, food, and medicine.[9] However, the babies kept dying not of infectious diseases or malnutrition but of a condition called *marasmus*. *Marasmus* is a Greek word that means "wasting away." The babies were dying because they lacked affection and physical touch, an incredibly important part of a human's sustenance.

Our God created us with the need to receive affection. When we don't get that affection, our body slowly starts wasting away.

Jesus demonstrated the power of touch and affection powerfully when He encountered a man who suffered from leprosy. Leprosy was considered a severe disease with many social and religious implications back in biblical times. Lepers were considered unclean and were often separated and cast away from their friends and family. It was believed that leprosy was contagious, and no one dared touch a person with leprosy.

The Bible recounts the story of a leper who broke the law. According to the Mosaic law, touching a leper was to become unclean. Yet, this man had been cast aside for a long time and likely knew the repercussions of breaking the law. Yet, when he heard that Jesus was passing by, he knelt and said, "If you are willing, you can make me clean." (Matthew 8:2). Now, Jesus had performed many miracles before this one. He could have said the words, and the man be healed. He could have sent the man to dip in a river and be healed. He could have done many creative things to heal this man.

Yet, He did the one thing that no one expected him to do. He reached out and *touched* the man. He gave the man what he needed to stop wasting away—human touch and affection, which in turn brought his physical healing.

Like this man who risked everything to get close to Jesus, we must do the same if we want to experience that healing.

Remember the story of the man who came to my university and told us we were all victims? In some way he was right. We have all been victims of something. And all those experiences have likely made us apprehensive and reluctant to be vulnerable, to open up. But there must come the point in our lives when we choose to run to Jesus and ask Him to heal us. A point where we learn to listen to His voice and all He has to say about us. A point where we learn to ignore the comments of those people who are only adding to our feelings of lack of self-worth and rejection.

That's what I decided to do in my own life and have experienced significant improvements. I won't say that I don't suffer from any feelings of rejection and low self-esteem. But I made it a priority to allow Jesus to work in me and have taken steps to eliminate the things that have caused me to feel negative about myself. All the steps discussed in the book I have put into practice. Apart from Jesus' healing, many other tools are available that can be of great help.

Today I am walking in the grace of God. I have allowed God to heal me, to restore me, to give me a new name and a new purpose. I have a beautiful family, a career, and a ministry.

Perhaps I need to remind you again that you are God's masterpiece, created by His excellence and formed according to His pleasure. Even your greatest flaws and most gruesome mistakes do not define you; the world's opinion should not limit you because you are who God says you are.

Jeremiah 1:5 reveals that before He formed you in the womb, He knew you, and before you were born, He set you apart and appointed you. Psalm 139:16 says, "His eyes saw your unformed body; all your days were written in His book and ordained for you before one of them came to be."

Maybe failed relationships, people's opinions, missed opportunities, and past disappointments have wounded your spirit, punctured your self-worth, and deflated your confidence. It is time to quit this valley of self-condemnation and allow God to work the course of your healing, freedom, and restoration. The world may be too busy to see the light you have in you. Their eyes may be clouded by the fog of perceived limitations around them, but God sees a victor and a winner rising already.

You are a work-in-progress and a champion in the making. He will wipe your tears of defeat and give you the joy of victory instead of the cry of despair.

He cares for you!

He says in His word: Fear not, for I am with you; be not dismayed, for I am your God; I will strengthen you, help you, and uphold you with my righteous hand (Isaiah 41:10).

Truth 8

God is willing and able to transform your life.
If you are willing, He will walk with you and
guide you during the process.

CHALLENGE 8

Are you willing to allow God to renew your mind? If yes, write down 3 practical steps you can take to start the process:

_____

_____

If no, what is stopping you?

_____

_____

The leper referenced in this chapter received healing when Jesus touched him. Can you identify what is missing in your life? What is that one thing that you need from Jesus?

_____

_____

We have value in God's eyes. Write down any two verses mentioned above and commit then to memory.

_____

_____

CONCLUSION

THE ROAD NOT TRAVELED

Humans are creatures of habit. We can get used to living a life of low self-esteem, living with feelings of unworthiness, and living as victims. We get so used to carrying around these things that we become comfortable with them.

In fact, many of us even become professional victims. There are certain perks that come along with being a victim. For example, people feel sorry for victims. People give victims a pass. We don't expect a lot from victims. The standard is lower, which means that as a victim, we don't have to work as hard because people are not expecting much from us.

It takes hard work to be a victor because as a victor you can no longer blame other people. You can no longer blame people for your actions. Now, you must own up to your mistakes. You must take responsibility for your choices. As victors we must own up to the consequences of our actions or inactions. This is the road less traveled.

What if you want to preserve the *status quo*? At this point you have lived your entire life this way. *Change is hard*, you say to yourself. And this is certainly one of the options. You can certainly continue holding on to your grudges, blaming everyone else for your failures, and hiding behind the security blanket that is the world of victimhood. But the years will go by, your bitterness will grow, and you might see everyone else around you succeed.

The next option is the hardest of the two. But you realize that standing still is not an option. Because while you're standing still the world is moving on without you. So, you decide that enough is enough. You decide that you are sick and tired of being sick and tired. You decide that you no longer want to proudly carry the banner of victimhood. You decide. You decide that from now on you will take responsibility for your own actions. You decide that you will do the work, even if it's hard, painful, and tiresome.

You take the road less traveled, but you know you are carving a new path. A new path for you, for your children, and the next generations to come. A path to victory.

END NOTES

(FOR MATURE AUDIENCE ONLY)

While I have discussed in this book the effects of different types of abuse, and the ways in which we can heal, I wanted to focus on sexual abuse specifically. Studies have shown that children who were victims of sexual abuse are prone to suffer from depression, guilt, shame, self-blame, eating disorders, somatic concerns, anxiety, dissociative patterns, repression, denial, sexual problems, and relationship problems.[10]

Every person is affected differently by sexual abuse. If you have been a victim of sexual abuse or know someone who has, you need to assess whether any of the areas above affect you. Once you have nailed down the specific areas, then you can narrow down your search for resources.

As I mentioned earlier, abuse tends to affect all areas of our lives. However, God in His love and mercy, has left us with people who can support us in our healing process.

Apart from the low self-esteem issues that I suffered since childhood, I also experienced other issues that I did not realize were problems until I became an adult. The biggest issue for me was constantly feeling ashamed of my body. I was never comfortable with my own body. Children who have been sexually abused often develop a negative body image due to being treated as sexual objects by their abusers during their formative years.

The second biggest issue was feeling uncomfortable with the male body. The word *uncomfortable* does not do it justice. For a long time, I detested the male body and did not find pleasure in sex.

It was obvious that these were areas where I needed help. Apart from the fact that sex was not enjoyable, it was also physically painful. I went to different gynecologists to see if there was anything physically wrong with me. Each checkup left me more confused since I didn't seem to have any physical problems.

After some research I came across with the term *vaginismus*.[11] Vaginismus is defined as "recurrent and persistent muscle spasms of the outer third of the vagina".[12] In essence, vaginismus occurs when the muscles of the vagina squeeze or spasm when something is entering it, like a tampon or a penis. Doctors don't know exactly why this happens. However, some studies have shown that there is a significant association between history of sexual abuse and vaginismus.[13]

The treatment for vaginismus seemed to help with

my physical pain. However, the body issues got better once I sought out professional help. My therapist, a God-fearing woman, used traditional therapy in conjunction with EMDR (Eye Movement Desensitization Reprocessing). After many sessions, the issues that I had with my own body and the male body diminished substantially.

Child sexual abuse is a significant problem. A couple of years after experiencing the first abuse, I suffered sexual abuse from a second male relative. By this time, I was sure that this was all my fault. After all, I didn't know anyone else that had experienced this. None of my friends had ever told me of anything like that happening to them. I was sure the abuse was all my fault. After all, what are the odds that I would be abused by two different people?

It wasn't until later in my life that I realized that child abuse is very common. In fact, about 1 in 4 girls and 1 in 13 boys in the United States experience child sexual abuse. What's most disturbing is that someone known and trusted by the child or child's family members, perpetrates 91% of child sexual abuse.[14]

Unfortunately, many survivors will go years without speaking out about their abuse and its consequences. However, speaking out can be a part of the healing process. Speaking up can help you to:

- Move through the guilt and secrecy that keeps you isolated.
- Move through denial and acknowledge the truth.
- Get the proper help.
- Get in touch with your feelings.
- Reclaim your voice.

- Join others who are no longer suffering in silence.
- End child sexual abuse by speaking up for others.
- Become a model for other survivors.

Then they cried to the LORD in their trouble, and he saved them from their distress.

PSALM 107:13

There is hope and healing in Christ! He is concerned with every area of our lives—even our sexual relationships.

APPENDIX

BIBLE VERSES

- Scripture quotations are listed in the order they appear in the book.
- When any Scripture reference is made in the book, the entire verse or passage is included here.
- Some verses are repeated.

CHAPTER 1

Now Naaman was commander of the army of the king of Aram. He was a great man in the sight of his master and highly regarded, because through him the LORD had given victory to Aram. He was a valiant soldier, but he had leprosy.

-2 Kings 5:1

CHAPTER 2

Then God said, "Let there be light," and there was light.

-Genesis 1:3

Then God said, "Let us make human beings in our image, to be like us. They will reign over the fish in the sea, the birds in the sky, the livestock, all the wild animals on the earth, and the small animals that scurry along the ground."

-Genesis 1:26

Then God said, "Let us make human beings in our image, to be like us. They will reign over the fish in the sea, the birds in the sky, the livestock, all the wild animals on the earth, and the small animals that scurry along the ground."

-James 3:9-11(NIV)

A man has joy by the answer of his mouth, And a word *spoken* in due season, how good *it is!*

-Proverbs 15:23(NKJV)

CHAPTER 3

So I have come down to rescue them from the power of the Egyptians and lead them out of Egypt into their own fertile and spacious land. It is a land flowing with milk and honey—the land where the Canaanites, Hittites, Amorites, Perizzites, Hivites, and Jebusites now live.

-Exodus 3:8

CHAPTER 5

But his officers tried to reason with him and said, "Sir,[a] if the prophet had told you to do something very difficult, wouldn't you have done it? So you should certainly obey him when he says simply, 'Go and wash and be cured!'"

-2 Kings 5:13

Trust in the LORD with all your heart,
And lean not on your own understanding;
In all your ways acknowledge Him,
And He shall direct your paths.
Do not be wise in your own eyes;
Fear the LORD and depart from evil.
It will be health to your flesh,
And strength to your bones.

-Proverbs 3:5-8(NKJV)

CHAPTER 6

But Moses pleaded with the LORD, "O Lord, I'm not very good with words. I never have been, and I'm not now, even though you have spoken to me. I get tongue-tied, and my words get tangled."

-Exodus 4:10

Moses was taught all the wisdom of the Egyptians, and he was powerful in both speech and action.

-Acts 7:22

Then the LORD asked Moses, "Who makes a person's mouth? Who decides whether people speak or do not speak, hear or do not hear, see or do not see? Is it not I, the LORD? Now go! I will be with you as you speak, and I will instruct you in what to say."

-Exodus 4:11-12

CHAPTER 7

Don't copy the behavior and customs of this world, but let God transform you into a new person by changing the way you think. Then you will learn to know God's will for you, which is good and pleasing and perfect.

-Romans 12:2

But to all who believed him and accepted him, he gave the right to become children of God.

-John 1:12

[W]ho purchased our freedom and forgave our sins.

-Colossians 1:14

Long ago the LORD said to Israel:
"I have loved you, my people, with an everlasting love.
 With unfailing love I have drawn you to myself.

-Jeremiah 31:3

Our lives are a Christ-like fragrance rising up to God. But this fragrance is perceived differently by those who are being saved and by those who are perishing.

-2 Corinthians 2:15

I no longer call you slaves, because a master doesn't confide in his slaves. Now you are my friends, since I have told you everything the Father told me.

-John 15:15

I no longer call you slaves, because a master doesn't confide in his slaves. Now you are my friends, since I have told you everything the Father told me.

-Colossians 3:12

For we are God's masterpiece. He has created us anew in Christ Jesus, so we can do the good things he planned for us long ago.

-Ephesians 2:10

And now, dear brothers and sisters, one final thing. Fix your thoughts on what is true, and honorable, and right, and pure, and lovely, and admirable. Think about things that are excellent and worthy of praise.

-Philippians 4:8

A prudent person foresees danger and takes precautions. The simpleton goes blindly on and suffers the consequences.

-Proverbs 22:3

Then Peter came to him and asked, "Lord, how often should I forgive someone who sins against me? Seven times?"

"No, not seven times," Jesus replied, "but seventy times seven!

-Matthew 18:21-22(NLT)

All of you together are Christ's body, and each of you is a part of it. Here are some of the parts God has appointed for the church:
first are apostles,
second are prophets,
third are teachers,
then those who do miracles,
those who have the gift of healing,
those who can help others,
those who have the gift of leadership,
those who speak in unknown languages.

-1 Corinthians 12:27-28 (NLT)

CHAPTER 8

For we are God's masterpiece. He has created us anew in Christ Jesus, so we can do the good things he planned for us long ago.

-Ephesians 2:10

So God created human beings in his own image.
  In the image of God he created them;
  male and female he created them.

-Genesis 1:27

So God created human beings in his own image.
  In the image of God he created them;
  male and female he created them.

-Exodus 19:5

"For this is how God loved the world: He gave his one and only Son, so that everyone who believes in him will not perish but have eternal life.

-John 3:16

We now have this light shining in our hearts, but we ourselves are like fragile clay jars containing this great treasure. This makes it clear that our great power is from God, not from ourselves.

-2 Corinthians 4:7

Suddenly, a man with leprosy approached him and knelt before him. "Lord," the man said, "if you are willing, you can heal me and make me clean."

-Matthew 8:2

"I knew you before I formed you in your mother's womb.
  Before you were born I set you apart
  and appointed you as my prophet to the nations."

-Jeremiah 1:5

You saw me before I was born.
  Every day of my life was recorded in your book.
Every moment was laid out
  before a single day had passed.

-Psalm 139:16

Don't be afraid, for I am with you.
  Don't be discouraged, for I am your God.
I will strengthen you and help you.
  I will hold you up with my victorious right hand.

-Isaiah 41:10

TRUTHS

Truth 1
Even through the bitter experiences,
God has a plan for you.

Truth 2
Words can either be fruit or poison

Truth 3
Past experiences may have distorted our
perception of ourselves

Truth 4
It's Not All About You

Truth 5
We often disqualify ourselves

Truth 6
People are often afraid to admit their
shortcomings and weaknesses.

Truth 7
We have all been victims of something but through
Christ we can find a path to victory

Truth 8
God is willing and able to transform your life.
If you are willing, He will walk with you
and guide you during the process.

REFERENCES

[1] Tony Evans, (2017). *Detours: The Unpredictable Path to Your Destiny*

[2] Phll Reed D.Phll, "Anxiety and Social Media Use", *Psychology Today* (February 3, 2020), www.psychologytoday.com/us/blog/digital-world-real-world/202002/anxiety-and-social-media-use

[3] Jon Hawkins, "Psychologically Speaking, the World Doesn't Revolve Around You", *Mind Café* (October 22, 2020), https://medium.com/mind-cafe/psychologically-speaking-the-world-doesnt-revolve-around-you-c52ab7dd0cec

[4] K.R. Harrison, (2014). *Victors and Victims*

[5] Craig Groeschel, (2021). *Winning the War in Your Mind: Change Your Thinking, Change Your Life*

[6] Priscilla Shirer, (2015). *The Armor of God*

[7] Henry Cloud and John Townsend, (1992). *Boundaries: When to Say Yes How to Say No to Take Control of Your Life*

[8] Johan Denollet, Susanne S. Pedersen

Anger, Depression, and Anxiety in Cardiac Patients

Journal of the American College of Cardiology, Volume 53, Issue 11, 17 March 2009, Pages 947-949

[9] Ben E. Benjamin, "The Primacy of Human Touch", *Health Touch News*, http://www.benbenjamin.com/pdfs/Issue2.pdf#:~:text=Ah undred%20years%20ago%2C%20about%2099%25%20of%20 babies%20in,were%20an%20everyday%20part%20of%20the %20social%20landscape.

[10] Hall, M., & Hall, J. (2011). The long-term effects of childhood sexual abuse: Counseling implications. Retrieved from http://counselingoutfitters.com/vistas/vistas11/Article_19.pdf

[11] Harish, Thippeswamy et al. "Successful management of vaginismus: An eclectic approach." Indian journal of psychiatry vol. 53,2 (2011): 154-5. doi:10.4103/0019-5545.82548

[12] https://www.smsna.org/patients/news/history-of-sexual-abuse-increases-the-risk-of-sexual-pain-in-women

[13] https://www.smsna.org/patients/news/history-of-sexual-abuse-increases-the-risk-of-sexual-pain-in-women

[14] www.cdc.gov/violenceprevention/childsexualabuse/fastfact.html

www.ingramcontent.com/pod-product-compliance
Lightning Source LLC
Chambersburg PA
CBHW032046040426
42449CB00007B/1001